101 ESSEI
ON MANAGIN(
THE SECONE

101 ESSENTIAL LISTS SERIES

101 Essential Lists for the Early Years – Penny Tassoni

101 Essential Lists for Primary Teachers – Fred Sedgwick

101 Essential Lists for Secondary Teachers – Susan Elkin

101 Essential Lists for Teaching Assistants – Louise Burnham

101 Essential Lists for SENCOs – Kate Griffiths and Jo Haines

101 Essential Lists for Using ICT in the Classroom – George Cole

101 Essential Lists on Assessment – Tabatha Rayment

101 Essential Lists on Managing Behaviour in the Secondary School –
Alex Griffiths and Pauline Stephenson

101 Essential Lists on Managing Behaviour in the Primary School –
Alex Griffiths and Karen Jones

101 Essential Lists for Managing Behaviour in the Early Years –
Simon Brownhill, Fiona Shelton and Clare Gratton

101 ESSENTIAL LISTS
ON MANAGING
BEHAVIOUR IN THE
SECONDARY SCHOOL

Alex Griffiths and Pauline Stephenson

Continuum International Publishing Group
The Tower Building   80 Maiden Lane
11 York Road   Suite 704
London   New York, NY 10038
SE1 7NX

www.continuumbooks.com

British Library Cataloguing-in-Publication Data
A catalogue record for this book is available from the British Library.

ISBN: 0-8264-8864-1 (paperback)

Library of Congress Cataloging-in-Publication Data
A catalog record for this book is available from the Library of Congress.

Typeset by YHT Ltd
Printed and bound in Great Britain by Ashford Colour Press, Gosport,
Hants

CONTENTS

National Strategy 1

Statistics on behaviour

Over the years government policy has attempted to improve behaviour and attendance in schools. However, many feel that behaviour is deteriorating and that classroom teachers face too many daily problems. A survey in 2004 by the Association of Teachers and Lecturers suggested some very major concerns:

- 85% of teachers believed that the National Curriculum, with all its restrictions, disengages young people from education and contributes to poor pupil behaviour.
- 72% of secondary school teachers had considered leaving the profession because of persistent disruptive behaviour by their pupils.
- 46% claimed to have suffered from some kind of mental health problem as a result of difficult pupil behaviour.
- 14% had been subjected to actual bodily harm.
- 39% of teachers were not satisfied with their school's behaviour policy.
- 74% were aware of colleagues who had left the profession, stating that the reason was essentially poor behaviour.
- 88% of teachers were not aware of any risk assessments being undertaken in their schools on students with a history of aggression.
- 61% of teachers felt that their schools should conduct risk assessments.

Nevertheless, there is much we can do for ourselves. We might envy those countries where 800 students sit and listen without a murmur, but is learning there really effective? So never feel alone; we all face the issue of managing behaviour while ensuring effective learning.

LIST 2   Remember, you are the teacher

'Disciplina' means teaching. We need to teach pupils to make better choices and to remember that:

- pupil behaviour usually communicates information about their needs
- many students do not know innately how to behave appropriately
- behaviour can be changed – it is not static or fixed – though sometimes it takes a while
- behaviour and its causes are complex concepts
- you are a teacher, not a social worker or psychotherapist
- many of us have not had the opportunity to develop our skills in the area of behaviour management
- if we want to change behaviour, sometimes we have to change our own behaviour first
- we don't just control others, we help them to control themselves
- we really can exacerbate or reduce the behaviours we encounter
- we should look after ourselves and in particular guarantee our own safety, as well as the safety of others
- no matter how good your behaviour control is, it can always be improved
- if you are having problems with an individual pupil or certain classes or even with the job generally, don't despair, because everything can improve
- help is available from colleagues, external agencies, government and local authority publications and from your own resources
- we all have good days and bad days
- you don't have to like or love every pupil, your job is to enable him or her to learn.

There have been many government initiatives over the years with regard to behaviour management. In 1989 the Elton Report was aimed at helping teachers and schools improve behaviour, and in December 2002 the Government set out to improve behaviour and attendance in schools. Both initiatives aimed to:

- make every school a place of inclusive learning in which pupils achieve their potential and have respect for others
- ensure that all children receive a high-quality education, including those who have been excluded or who have fallen out of the education system, and to engage pupils and parents more actively in behaviour and attendance
- improve behaviour generally and reduce truancy.

As a key part of the Government's strategy, The Behaviour Improvement Programme (BIP) was launched. This provided:

- multi-agency teams (BESTs) to help some schools. If there is a BEST team operating in your school you could well have extra access to police officers and behaviour specialists
- keyworkers for all pupils at risk of exclusion, truancy and criminal behaviour
- full-time, supervised education for all excluded pupils
- possible access (via the multi-disciplinary teams) to educational psychologists, clinical psychologists, speech and language therapists, social workers, education welfare officers, family liaison officers, behaviour support staff, health visitors, school nurses and mental health workers.

This is all very well, but in the end you are on your own in the classroom with a group of youngsters who can cause you problems! Government policy is fine, but what you really need are down-to-earth, practical, easy-to-implement strategies to enable you to cope from Monday to Friday!

Top tip: However good you are you can always be better.

Understanding Challenging Behaviour

 ## What is challenging behaviour?

The press, the media generally and the gossips in our neighbourhood would have us believe that challenging behaviour:

○ is shown by children with severe learning or emotional difficulties who are 'running riot'
○ happens because parents are struggling to manage their children's behaviour and can't even get them to go to school
○ is due to poor parenting skills which is leading to the breakdown of law and order in our local community
○ is the fault of teachers, headteachers and schools!

We used to talk of disruptive behaviour, and many tomes were written on the subject, but now we use the word 'challenge', and it need not refer to severe misdeeds or problems. Challenge is a new pc word that means something is difficult and in some way not really wanted or expected. Challenging behaviours are all those low-level as well as high-level behaviours that interfere in some way with teaching and learning, thus making it less efficient and effective.

LIST 5 Examples of challenging behaviour

- Talking in class
- Verbal abuse
- Interrupting or bothering other pupils
- Teasing other students
- Asking unnecessary questions
- Not settling to work
- Not using equipment properly
- Not listening to the teacher
- Daydreaming
- Refusing to work
- Failing to complete homework assignments
- Not finishing class assignments
- Damaging property
- Arriving late for lessons
- Not sitting in a seat
- Complaining
- Aggressive or inappropriate body language
- Excessive talking
- Threats of (or real) violence
- Failing to work effectively
- Preventing others from working
- Being noisy
- Silent insolence
- Swearing
- Anything that can irritate and stop the flow of a well-prepared lesson
- Any behaviour which increases your blood pressure, drives you to alcohol or cigarettes, makes you bad tempered with your best friend or partner or generally stops you from enjoying your evening or weekend!

LIST 6 Possible causes

Common causes of challenging behaviour from students include:

- ○ sheer boredom in a lesson for whatever reason
- ○ the work takes too long
- ○ not able to do the work set
- ○ not being or feeling valued
- ○ not being or feeling able to contribute
- ○ not understanding what has to be done
- ○ seeking attention from the teacher or others
- ○ poor self-esteem
- ○ finding no reward in the situation.

LIST 7   Factors affecting behaviour

You will have noticed that a student's mood and behaviour can swing, sometimes quite suddenly. Even school events can cause minor disturbance as routines change. Think how the following may alter students' – or even your – behaviour.

- A new class in September
- Finding the way around a new school
- Old friends no longer around
- New rules with new teachers
- Standard Assessment Tests (SATs) and allied pressures
- The run up to and just after holiday and half-term breaks
- The clocks changing
- A very windy day
- Snow
- Ice or rain
- Big local events, such as carnivals
- Bonfire night, Christmas, Easter
- Tiredness as the term progresses
- Preparation for exams
- Mock and real exams
- Reports and report writing
- The aftermath of parents' evenings
- School events, such as sports day
- Preparing to move class
- A late night mid-week.

L I S T 8 — Your role in ensuring good behaviour

The word 'discipline' often conjures up images of punishment but think of it as a means to promote learning, rather than punishment for wrongdoings. Here are some points to note about your role in applying discipline and promoting good behaviour.

- ○ Discipline can be imposed on students by others but can also come from within the student.
- ○ As educators it is important we teach students to be able to self-discipline. When students leave home or go on to higher education, those who have self-discipline will be able to cope, whereas those used to imposed discipline will find everything much more difficult.
- ○ If parents and teachers are too permissive, students can fail to develop a good work ethic. Excessive freedom is not a precursor to good learning. You will know students who, if given freedom to choose their workload, would opt for doing very little!
- ○ Middle ground is required between the punitive and the permissive styles of teaching, as students like to know where they stand and what to expect.
- ○ Consistency is the key – it is confusing to be reprimanded for something while another person receives no reprimand for the same apparent transgression.
- ○ Each environment has expectations and expected types of behaviour. We all like to feel safe and secure and have adapted to varying environments and different sets of rules. Think what it is like when your routine becomes disrupted. No cornflakes at breakfast, no sugar at school breaktime and woe betide anybody who gets in the way of your first caffeine fix.
- ○ Students vary in temperament and, like you, can be subject to a variety of emotions. Your own emotions can vary considerably within one school day.
- ○ Students bring their own problems to school. They may be the sole carer for a parent or sibling, the child of an alcoholic parent, involved in a drug culture or up till the early hours watching inappropriate films. They may have struggled to find any appropriate clothing to wear for school or simply be used to doing what they want, when they want.

○ We must aim for peace in the classroom, both for our charges and for ourselves.

LIST 9 Your teaching skills

Challenging behaviour can partially be addressed by careful planning and constant evaluation of students' work and progress. There are several points you need to consider.

- Our behaviour influences the behaviour of our pupils.
- Strategies and techniques to improve our classroom management can be identified and learned.
- Each of us needs to take responsibility for developing our skills.
- Improved effectiveness will minimize our problems.
- Over-disciplining can be counter productive.
- Non-stop nit-picking or bombarding students with negative comments is doomed to failure.
- It is important that a student realizes that you've noticed one positive rather than all the negatives.
- Save time and energy for worthwhile causes and try to avoid those situations where you are not likely to get a desirable outcome.
- We should not be ruthless risk-takers who use power and threats to make students do what we want.
- We should create options in case we can't reach an agreement, as this will prevent us from settling on an undesirable outcome.
- We should ask lots of questions, listen carefully and so build rapport and trust.
- The best solutions for all may not be immediately evident. We must stay flexible and think creatively.
- Once a student has been sanctioned for a behaviour then we should not refer to it again.
- We should never let trivial occurrences escalate out of all proportion.
- We should not make one-way concessions. If we give a little, they should give a little too.
- If you have always entered 8F with dread, it is time to change your attitude. If your mind-set indicates you will have a bad day, then you most certainly will. Always be positive, even on Friday afternoon.
- Our main aim should be to have a peaceful classroom.

Top tip: Never ever criticize the person, only the behaviour.

Policies, Rules and Responsibilities 3

LIST 10 — Effective strategies

A recent review of strategies for promoting positive behaviour in Scottish schools found that the following general approaches to managing behaviour and discipline are particularly effective:

- The school has clear expectations, communicates positively and regularly, and the policies are implemented consistently by all staff across the whole school.
- All staff are highly visible and challenge inappropriate behaviour wherever and whenever they encounter it.
- There is consistent use of praise to recognize and encourage good behaviour.
- Dress codes are implemented to introduce a sense of school identity and pride.
- Students are involved in decision-making and forums exist for pupils to complain, e.g. student councils.
- There are opportunities for students to take responsibility for others through schemes such as the 'buddying' or mentoring of younger pupils.
- There is recognition and celebration of success in behaviour, as well as achievement.
- There are opportunities to discuss behaviour-related issues during personal and social education classes.
- All sanctions and rewards are clearly understood and consistently implemented.
- Staff are given practical advice on implementing care and welfare policies, including policies on child protection, anti-bullying and racial equality, as well as on promoting positive behaviour.
- Behaviour also improves when additional staff are deployed to support pupils in class and at breaks.

Your school behaviour policy

Every school should have a behaviour policy, so find out what yours says. The DfES website provides suggestions for drafting such a policy – see www.standards.dfes.gov.uk/keystage3.

All policies should be developed through discussion to encourage ownership. There should be discussion on:

○ the school ethos
○ the current effectiveness of the school and its procedures
○ how to run the school efficiently to encourage learning
○ what values and beliefs are held about behaviour
○ the need for all to keep rigidly to any policy.

As a minimum the policy should:

○ cover the routines in learning and teaching that govern the school day
○ emphasize achievement and success
○ establish shared and possibly individual rewards
○ specify clear sanctions and punishments
○ refer to bullying
○ emphasize that the school will be a safe place
○ comment on the responsibility and involvement of parents
○ take account of equal opportunity for all
○ refer to the procedures to establish these issues.

Reviewing your policy

Your school behaviour policy should be:

○ reviewed regularly
○ strictly adhered to by all staff, whatever their views
○ changed when changes occur within the school
○ considered in the light of child protection issues.

If you are unhappy about any aspect of the policy then you must:

○ consult with your line manager
○ bring the issue up at staff meetings
○ encourage debate in the staffroom
○ always abide by the policy until it is changed.

A policy is only as strong as its weakest link. Make sure you are not the weak link! Find out from the policy and from colleagues:

○ what training is available on behaviour management
○ what support systems are in place to deal with the more challenging behaviours
○ how the school obtains additional support, e.g. has the school a directory of support services and a list of procedures for securing additional support?
○ where the staff handbook (which should be extensive and comprehensive) is kept
○ what the school's policy is about teachers contacting parents
○ how a student is referred to the learning support unit
○ how a student is referred to other services, such as an educational psychologist or educational social or welfare worker.

Checklist for creating a policy

Use this checklist as an aide-memoire when designing or revisiting a whole-school behaviour and attendance policy.

- What are the principles behind the school policy?
- In what way do they apply to each and every member of the school?
- Are the aims of the school compatible with the principles of the policy?
- Do the principles relate appropriately to the school curriculum?
- In what ways does the policy promote positive learning?
- Does it promote positive but also effective teaching?
- In what ways does it encourage attendance?
- Consider everyone's role (including governors') to see if the policy promotes positive behaviour.
- How are rewards and sanctions used to encourage positive behaviour generally?
- Does the policy set high standards for behaviour?
- What support systems or facilities are available to help students who have learning, personal or family difficulties?
- What are the support and training arrangements for staff?
- How are parents supported, and how can they be given information to help them to be more effective and supportive to their children and the school?
- Is everyone, including parents, involved in producing the policy?
- What resources – financial as well as personal – are put into ensuring that the policy is effective?
- How will the policy be monitored to ensure that it remains effective?

LIST 14   Key areas for class rules

Every school needs a behaviour policy and every classroom should have its rules. There are six key areas for classroom rule-making:

- Communication
- Learning
- Movement
- Personal problem-solving
- General code of conduct
- Safety.

Each rule that is agreed will:

- need to be fully discussed with the class
- be age appropriate for the class
- be presented in a suitable way
- require defining as exactly as possible
- need to be taught and learnt in the same way as other curriculum areas
- need reviewing with the class during the year to make appropriate changes
- need to be displayed so that it can be pointed to
- be consistent with general school rules
- not upset colleagues, your headteacher or parents
- meet the needs and demands of your classroom and your subject.

It is usually not a good idea to hold in-depth discussions about sanctions for breaking the rules. Young people can devise wicked punishments you cannot use!

LIST 15   Implementing the rules

Frequent rule-breaking is avoided by frequent rule discussions, so:

- Keep the emphasis on positive behaviour
- Start as you mean to go on – work on rules at the beginning of term
- Keep the list clear
- Keep the list brief
- Make the rules as user-friendly as you can
- Emphasize rewards
- Put 'In our classroom' before each rule to personalize it
- Put your name in the list to make it even more personal
- Include any special rules
- Ensure that there is no 'rule-bending'
- Ask questions rather than simply repeat the rules
- Make sure that any routines are practised
- Do dry runs for occasional events, such as fire practice
- If you have had any difficulty, mention the rules at the beginning of new lessons
- Praise and sanction any good examples of behaviour and infringements.

Examples of class rules

Here are some examples of possible rules in each of the key areas (see List 14 Key areas for class rules).

Communication

- When we wish to ask questions we will put up our hand and wait our turn.
- We will talk quietly when we are working.
- We will never talk when the teacher is talking.
- We will use kind language.
- We will allow and help everyone to learn.
- We will respect the right of our teacher to teach.
- When learning we will need to work quietly, help others and share equipment.
- We will respect other people's opinions.
- We will listen to instructions.

Movement

- When we have to get out of our chair we will ask our teacher by putting our hand up and waiting for permission.
- We will ask permission to get out of our seat only if it is really necessary.
- If we get out of our seat, we will move quietly and try not to disturb others.

Personal problem-solving

- When we have a problem with another person we will try and sort it out quickly and quietly on our own.
- If we cannot settle our problems like this we will ask the teacher for help.
- We will settle our problems without the use of verbal or physical abuse or aggression.

Treatment – code of conduct

- We will try to treat everyone fairly.
- We will not comment on looks or clothes.

- We will respect each other's homes, religions and countries of birth.
- We will keep our hands, feet and possessions to ourselves.

Safety

- To be safe, we will walk and not run around our classroom.
- We will look after, and return, all equipment.

LIST 17 Your responsibilities

It should go without saying that poor behaviour can be avoided by doing all those things that a good teacher should do. So:

- Plan, prepare and organize well.
- Have accepted classroom routines, rules and regulations and stick to them.
- Organize yourself and the materials in your classroom.
- Look at seating arrangements.
- Ensure that work is differentiated and the content appropriate.
- Keep the self-esteem of pupils high.
- Be first into the classroom.
- Look authoritative by standing in a central position.
- Give lots of eye contact and scan the class, especially at the beginning of a lesson.
- Thwart any trouble by acting quickly in a low-level way, e.g. using eye contact or moving closer.
- Use names and define the unwanted behaviour and the required behaviour.
- Make corrective statements short, and move on.
- Be a good role model.
- Seek help from others if you need it.
- Accept you are not perfect and that things can go wrong for you!

Top tip: Remember: rights lead to responsibilities which lead to the need for rules.

Encouraging Good Behaviour

LIST 18 — Preparing for success

Good preparation will pay dividends in the long term.

- Your students have a greater chance of success and thus less incentive to misbehave.
- There should be no excuses about homework being unclear.
- Good planning leads to greater efficiency in so many ways.
- Differentiated worksheets can be used again at some future date (with some updating).
- Good resources (especially ICT) make for easier lesson planning.

Your students are more likely to succeed and be happy in school if they:

- feel valued and respected by staff and peers
- are treated fairly
- feel safe and secure
- see consistency at work in school at every level
- experience strategies that make learning interesting and dynamic
- feel that the work is set at the right level for them
- have the chance to participate in a peer mediation or conflict resolution programme in school
- have the opportunity to use peer-support or pupil-mentorship schemes in school
- are able to participate in a school council or other decision-making forum
- have opportunities for learning outside the formal setting of the classroom
- are provided with high standards of teaching and learning.

L I S T 19   Promoting positive behaviour

Consider some of these things you could do in your classroom to promote positive behaviour.

- ○ Define the good behaviour you require – have clear guidelines.
- ○ Define bad behaviour, with reasons if necessary.
- ○ Display classroom rules and school rules.
- ○ Remind students frequently of the rules.
- ○ Consistently follow agreed procedures.
- ○ Encourage a calm and quiet atmosphere.
- ○ Foster a work ethic in your class.
- ○ Look at class size and composition (if you have any control over this) and its relevance to behaviour.
- ○ Consider having no-go zones in your classroom, especially in dangerous areas, bearing age in mind.
- ○ Group students carefully.
- ○ Use distraction as a management tool.
- ○ Always set achievable targets.
- ○ Use negotiation rather than authoritarian approaches.
- ○ Deflect difficult situations gently as soon as you see them coming.
- ○ Try always to reinforce good behaviour.
- ○ Record positive and negative incidents.
- ○ Always criticize the behaviour, never the person – whatever you feel.
- ○ Use an agreed reward system and supplement this if it is helpful.
- ○ Ensure sanctions are understood and meaningful and not rewarding (like playing a computer game while on a detention-type activity).
- ○ Use privileges to encourage good behaviour.
- ○ Use very public and/or private praise regularly and often, but make sure that it is not patronizing to the student.
- ○ Praise/reward individual acts.
- ○ Praise/reward group or class acts.
- ○ Use photographs to promote self-esteem.
- ○ Encourage students to report the positive actions of others.
- ○ Continually analyze your class management and be prepared to make changes.

Keeping the peace

Here are some more strategies for ensuring positive behaviour in your school.

- Be seen as fair and always keep an open mind.
- Listen carefully to students before taking action – if necessary ensure that you have both 'calmed down'.
- Listen carefully to parents and give them time to tell their side of the story – if they have their chance to talk they are more likely to listen carefully to you.
- Contact home by telephone or letter when giving positive as well as negative messages. Follow up negative communications with positive ones (a real and regular complaint of parents).
- Make sure that parents know the rules and the reasoning behind them and involve parents generally.
- Use parent–teacher association (PTA) meetings to discuss positive approaches.
- Become involved in organizing learning events with parents to model good relationships.
- Lay on lunchtime activities to reduce opportunities for poor behaviour and organize extra-curricula activities.
- If you are a senior member of staff, be seen around the school.
- Be prepared to explain and discuss.
- Be prepared to ask others for assistance.
- If you make contracts with students, ensure that you have to give and not just take.
- Follow a good marking policy.
- Read the bullying policy.
- Read the restraint policy, if this is likely to be an issue.
- Read the equal opportunities policy.
- Move forward in a focused way, using small steps.

Transitions and unexpected events

Keep an eye out for all transition periods – it is these that can cause most difficulty. This is particularly true for those likely to display unruly or panicky behaviour at such times. Unexpected changes can also disrupt carefully laid plans. Some examples include:

- class changes.
- practice or real fire alarms
- an epileptic fit
- visitors to the classroom
- equipment not working
- a power cut
- light bulb failure
- sudden register checks
- furniture breaking
- teaching assistant illness.

This list could go on forever. The trick is to be prepared for as many of these as possible. Some may even be practised or at least discussed, thus generally encouraging good behaviour.

Top tip: Be well prepared and prepared to change.

Classroom Management

Student expectations

Our students have high expectations of us as teachers. They expect that we:

- give interesting, even exciting, lessons
- provide good explanations
- always treat them with respect
- are fair to everyone in the classroom
- are friendly and, preferably, likeable
- have an infallible sense of humour
- keep order in the classroom as a matter of routine
- dress appropriately
- run good end-of-term events
- ensure that they don't look silly at sports events
- make sure that they get their lunch on time
- keep them safe.

To do this, our lessons should be well prepared and organized and we should pay attention to each phase of a lesson. There are various phases to all lessons and this applies to almost any supervised activity, including lunch breaks.

Critical lesson points

- The entry and settling of the group
- The main lesson/activity
- Clear-up time
- Final exit.

Each phase has to be considered, and things to look at include:

- routines
- simplicity

- commonly accepted actions
- predictability for students
- common expectations.

Getting the entry to a situation right will alleviate many difficulties. The routine for your students should be simple and predictable. You are then very definitely in charge of your domain. Something different every time could be a recipe for disaster! But judge your group.

○ Dress in a manner that conveys you care enough about your appearance to make an effort for them, that you like to be clean and smart, and while you may not be wealthy you can still look good.

○ Ensure that you arrive at the classroom before your students. Unfortunately, this is not always possible so have a rule to ensure order, e.g. line up outside the class in an orderly way.

○ Consider the temperature of the room – it can influence behaviour. The lesson may be improved by opening windows and making sure that the atmosphere is not stuffy.

○ If the students enter noisily, then send them out again. Make them wait quietly, and line up in an orderly way. Stand silently, making eye contact with anyone talking or not conforming. Wait for quiet, then give clear, concise instructions for them to enter the room. Comment on any improved performance by the class. If there is a problem, repeat the process.

○ If there are issues, try a different seating arrangement. Look for random assignments rather than any choice on the part of the students. Try to ensure that there are no gaps in the middle of the classroom seating arrangement. When moving students, consider moving those at the back towards the front or middle of the classroom.

LIST 24 Successful entry techniques

Effective teachers always know what is happening in their classroom, and from the moment the students enter the room they are in control. They:

○ greet students as they enter the classroom
○ place themselves in a central position, so demonstrating their authority
○ always wait for silence before speaking
○ issue any directions with authority
○ teach class rules systematically
○ utilize good aids to give effective explanations
○ use eye contact continually (the proverbial 'eyes in the back of the head')
○ always respond quickly to any inappropriate behaviour
○ give feedback to individuals and the class on learning and behaviour
○ keep contact with the whole class, using their eyes and body
○ have detailed accountability systems for themselves and their students.

So, consider your class entry techniques, including general greeting and your speed of response to any difficulty (a look will often suffice, no need for more).

Once you have them in the classroom, how can you ensure that you have their attention?

- Make sure that the activity and the language you use matches student age and developmental level – attention is much greater when students fully understand what is required.
- Give information in concise, clear sentences and check frequently for understanding.
- Always prepare students for change, e.g. say, 'We have just finished doing that chart, now we are going to do a slightly different type of chart.'
- Keep unstructured time to a minimum as it leads to inattention.
- Structure activities so that there is little room for error. Success or the expectation of success enhances attention.
- If a student or group of students is struggling, provide additional information quickly, e.g. provide detail as to where to find information within a chapter or on a page.
- Publicly praise students who are attending to their work, and model good attention in your interactions.
- Remember, students work at different rates, and apparent inattention may only be reflecting this. Intervention at an early stage may only lower self-esteem, thus sowing the seed for future challenging behaviour.
- Encourage good listening skills by structuring your instructions and indicating what might be expected of the student following these.

LIST 26   Tips to maintain attention

○ Try to use pictures, diagrams or other visual aids to help verify and clarify the verbal instructions.

○ When talking, monitor how quickly you are speaking. This helps to control the amount of information you are expecting the students to understand. Do not overwhelm them with too many directives and explanations at any one time.

○ Present new information in short, meaningful chunks.

○ Try to include materials that are attractive or fresh for students.

○ Use lighting to focus attention, e.g. try turning off the lights except for those which cover the area in which you are working.

○ If you are given a classroom which has extremely poor lighting or problematic acoustics, ask if you can be timetabled into another room.

○ Change your tone of voice to enhance student interest.

○ Develop active participation strategies to maintain auditory attention. Ask regular questions which require a verbal answer or a physical response such as a thumbs-up or thumbs-down sign.

○ Try to reduce distractions in your classroom. Strategies such as ensuring that students with attention problems cannot look out of the window can be very helpful. Sometimes it is useful to have these students sitting close to you.

LIST 27 Dealing with attention difficulties

Some students find paying attention to the teacher particularly problematic. So,

○ Try to identify students with an attention problem early in the school year. This can only increase your chances of success.

○ If a particular student has attention difficulties, place them with a group of attentive, harder working, quiet students.

○ Allow students sufficient time to process fully any information you give them before asking for a response. If you feel that a student has not been paying attention to you, ask a low-level question rather than a question that is likely to confuse them. This brings them back, but avoids any follow-up behavioural difficulty.

○ Ensure you are close to a student when giving specific personal directions or instructions – this always aids attention.

○ Ask the student to repeat your request in their own words to check that they know exactly what to do. Make sure you allow enough time for completion of the task.

○ Focus a student's attention by saying their name at the beginning of the request.

○ Prompt a student to pay attention to you. You could verbally request that they listen, tap them very gently on the arm, wave to get their visual attention, or put your hand on their desk.

○ Have a short 'quiet time' for the whole group and then ask a student to list the sounds they heard. This helps develop listening skills.

○ When giving instructions, focus on telling the student what they can and not what they can't do.

○ Make sure there are no distracting items on the desk.

○ Have an agreement with specific individuals that a special sign, possibly known only to them, will be used to encourage attention.

○ If a student is working on a complex or difficult worksheet, use highlighters or outline the area of concern.

○ Use tape recorders and computers with headphones to aid concentration, listening and understanding.

○ Try to use language such as 'What are you supposed to be doing?', 'How are you getting on?', 'Are you nearing the end of the first part of this?' This can encourage concentration on the task at hand.

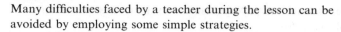

LIST 28   The main lesson

Many difficulties faced by a teacher during the lesson can be avoided by employing some simple strategies.

- Outline the general lesson plan to the students, thus making the future more predictable.
- Ensure that everything is ready, so mischief-makers don't have the time or space to make mischief.
- Know each student's name – this is essential, especially if you are covering a lesson for someone else.
- Give praise liberally and be courteous, but do it honestly.
- Plan and prepare the tasks, including special tasks for particular students.
- Be specific about tasks new to the class.
- Walk around the classroom while the students are working, refer to them by name and comment positively on their work. Let them observe that you are interested in them as people and in the work they are doing, and that you are monitoring how much work they are doing. Regularly encourage them to do a little more.
- Don't interrupt an individual's work. While working they are not causing trouble. When they stop, praise them for the work they have done and move them on to the next task. This will help develop a work ethos.
- Resolve issues as quickly and fairly as possible.

LIST 29   Responding to interruptions

Respond quickly to any interruptions, no matter how minor.

○ Give an old-fashioned, authoritative stare – we all know this one and we all do it slightly differently. Develop yours and let it become your feature of disapproval, but try not to overdo it as you will soon be mimicked.

○ Ask a low-key question, so you don't put anyone on the spot. This brings attention back to the subject and away from their neighbour.

○ Use student names to make comment as this personalizes the interaction and demonstrates some care on your part about them and their behaviour.

○ Always focus on the behaviour not the person. Avoid 'You are a naughty...', use instead 'That behaviour is not acceptable.'

○ Explain any unequal treatment to stop any festering gossip. Equality is difficult to ensure and inequality is sometimes the best way to develop better behaviour. Explain to the group why certain sanctions or rewards have been administered and you may well find you will be given the support of the whole group.

○ Talk about the effect on the curriculum and not the behaviour as this helps students to focus on the reasons for being in the class.

○ Loud rebukes can sometimes be effective but only if used rarely, otherwise rebuke in private. A loud noise followed by silence will gradually silence a noisy group but allow time for the group to appreciate fully what is required. Look after your voice – it is your living.

○ An effective intervention is abrupt, short and doesn't invite further comment.

○ Maintain the structure of your lesson until the very end.

○ Determine the tasks for this time, including how and when you want things done and who should be involved.

○ Give clear, concise instructions.

○ Describe the expected behaviour as accurately as possible, e.g. 'Put the weathercocks away, then sit down quietly.'

○ Remember that your exit is someone else's start, so orderly exits are important. You may get the blame for later difficulties.

○ Have a clear routine and system for dismissal. Use the last seconds to reinforce good behaviour. It is a moment of special power! They want to move on and avoid trouble elsewhere and will work together to ensure this. Don't abuse these moments, as they are brief, but give comment and praise quickly.

○ Keep the troublemaker back for a few moments only – this will be enough to disrupt his/her effect on others and disadvantages them when joining the rest of the group. And you would not want to miss your caffeine break, would you?

LIST 31 What to do when trouble starts!

Here are some simple early interventions to use at the first sign of trouble.

❍ Whenever you are intervening always allow 'take-up time'. This allows students a little while to take in, understand and put into action your requests. Give them the opportunity to weigh up the consequences of their actions.

❍ Be confident in any action you take.

❍ Never be confrontational – this will always 'set you up for a fight'.

❍ Never invade personal space and keep a reasonable distance at all times – no finger-wagging or face-to-face confrontations.

❍ Always appear calm and look as though you are in charge, even if you don't feel it – this is the key to success.

❍ Once the interaction is over, do not refer to it again unless it re-occurs shortly afterwards.

❍ When interacting with your class, take up any issues as quickly as possible so that you can get on with the lesson.

❍ Try 'the pause', 'Gareth (short pause), listen please. Thank you.' Try to model courtesy in all your interactions.

❍ Give the student choice, 'Kylie, what do we do when collecting the books?' or 'Either put it away or you can give it to me.' Don't expect immediate compliance.

❍ Partial agreement can help. Faced with a comment such as, 'You're not the headteacher', your reply could be, 'You're right, but I am responsible for you during lunchtime.' Or, 'William, face this way and listen please. Thanks.' 'But I'm only drawing the picture.' 'Maybe you were and now I want you to face this way and listen.'

❍ State the rule, 'Mary, we have a rule for asking questions and I expect you to use it. Thanks.'

If you find your initial intervention is not working you will need to take further action.

○ Don't merely repeat instructions, but increase their seriousness, as in, 'Josephine, face this way, thanks', then, 'Josephine, the instruction is face this way and listen. Thank you.' And finally, 'Josephine, if you choose to ignore my instructions then you are choosing to talk to me for two minutes at breaktime.'

○ Have a quiet word, sometimes called 'conferencing'. Kneel, stoop or bend down to student level and quietly and briefly make your point. This strategy does not reduce self-esteem by making public statements; it removes the audience and thus other potential problems, gives personal attention and makes very clear your expectation. This type of almost final intervention tends to lead to compliance.

○ Give a choice, 'If you choose not to finish your work before break then you're choosing to finish it at lunchtime. Your choice, which is it to be?' (Give take-up time before following it through.)

○ If a student or class is proving particularly difficult for you, first ensure that there really is a problem. Defining the exact behaviour that you are concerned about easily does this. All you need to do then is to count the number of times it happens in a lesson – or in a day. You may well find that the problem is not as serious as you think it is.

LIST 33   Rules for interventions

- ○ Try to keep the flow of the lesson going.
- ○ Use low-level techniques initially, such as a glance or a stare, and if you are in full flow, move closer to the 'offender'. Use techniques such as partial agreement to have a civilized, well-modelled interaction.
- ○ Try to give the student choices which direct them to what you want them to do.
- ○ Allow them take-up time to assimilate your request, make a decision and put it into operation.
- ○ Remember: give the instruction, remind them of this, then give a choice.
- ○ Don't repeat yourself but increase the 'seriousness' of your language.
- ○ Consider having a quiet word.
- ○ Be fair, consistent, polite and generally treat a student as you would wish to be treated, even in a problematic situation.

Top tip: Remember to give choice and take-up time – essential for avoiding and dealing with any trouble.

Common Class Problems 6

LIST 34 — Unfinished work

Many classes have several or more students who do not finish their work.

- Discuss the issue with the students.
- You could whinge at them – but that can be tedious.
- Make sure the work is within their capability.
- Find a time to assess how much a student can do while being 'watched' – this will help you set a target for them.
- Think of a reward for them if they finish work on time – discuss possibilities with them.
- You could design a daily chart, giving a tick for each successful lesson. A reward is given after an agreed number of successful lessons on the trot (keep the number low or it won't be achieved, e.g. three lessons).
- Decide what is to be done about the non-completion of work, e.g. give it as a homework assignment. In severe cases, consider a phone call to parents to back this up.
- Congratulate success.

Interruptions during explanations

- Discuss the rule with the class.
- Discuss the problem that has arisen in terms of students not understanding all the instructions, as interruptions have led to confusion.
- Indicate when you will not expect any interruption during an explanation.
- Decide on a class reward if there are no interruptions.
- Decide with the class on a consequence for failure to comply.
- Stick to it.

Dealing with hypochondria

Some students continually complain about their health. This means they work less and set a poor example for others.

○ Determine from a good source whether the student does have a health problem or not.

○ If there is a problem, take it into consideration when determining what you expect, e.g. slow the pace for them.

○ If there is no known problem, send the student to be checked every time they complain.

○ Do not comment or give any sympathy – just send them for a check-up.

○ Make it clear to the student that any time lost by being checked will need to be made up.

○ Explain everything to the student, including exactly why you are taking this action which is effectively ignoring the unwanted behaviour.

○ Remember, this may be attention-seeking behaviour so give attention when the student is working well.

○ If it is a self-image issue, give positive messages about the student and build them up in any area you can.

○ Ask other teachers to do the same.

LIST 36 Are you picking on them?

You may well come across a student who complains you are picking on them during class time.

○ Ask yourself whether this is actually fair comment. If it is, do something about it.

○ If it is not (more than likely!), consider discussing complaints in the class. Do this in free or study time or near the end of a lesson in case it unleashes hell and other furies.

○ If there is a problem with a particular student, arrange for them to come and see you at designated times to discuss problems they have with you – encourage this, explaining that you want to be fair to everyone.

○ Explain that any complaints about you, your teaching or your subject should be discussed at such times only.

○ Then ignore any complaining in class, reminding them of the agreed discussion times.

○ Go out of your way (but not too far) to make positive comments to the complainer, demonstrating your interest in them and their future success.

LIST 37 Simple tactics for individual students

Here are some simple ways of helping individual students.

The student who quickly lashes out at any criticism

- Explain that when we are angry we breathe with sharp, short breaths and to calm down we need to breathe more slowly.
- Ask them to try taking short but deep breaths when they feel angry.
- Get them to breathe in while they count to five and to breathe out counting to five.
- Ask them to practise this and use it when they are angry – with any luck it will keep them out of trouble.

The frustrated or angry student

- Ask them to write down why they are angry or frustrated.
- Pick up any issues and discuss them.
- Encourage them to get rid of their frustrations.
- Persuade them to screw up the paper they have written on, throw it in the bin and then forget all about it.

The cheeky student

- When faced with cheekiness, the important point is not to engage in a discussion.
- A withering look often works if the cheekiness cannot obviously be ignored.
- Sometimes a humorous retort, if you are quick enough, will put you back in the driving seat.
- Changing the subject can also help.

Some common examples:

- If a student asks about a rude term, respond with, 'That is not relevant now, you can look it up later.'
- If you are called by your first name, reply, 'I'm sure people know my first name but in the classroom I want to be known as. . .'
- If a student makes a derogatory comment, such as 'fat slob', say, 'We are not getting into a discussion on physical features now.'

In essence, move the conversation on and away from the cheeky comment.

Top tip: Never wade in when a lower-level strategy will suffice.

Language

7

Common expressions

We all say things we think everyone else will understand. Shared understanding is one aspect of language that we too often take for granted. Some students with language processing difficulties fail to grasp what we are saying, while others only process at a superficial level, and some process what we say absolutely literally.

Look at these sayings and contemplate what they really mean and what we are actually saying!

- ❍ It's raining cats and dogs.
- ❍ What time do you call this?
- ❍ Take a seat.
- ❍ Can you give me a hand?
- ❍ Pull your socks up.
- ❍ Put your best foot forward.
- ❍ I'm feeling on top of the world.
- ❍ Would you like to help me?
- ❍ Can you give the pencils out?
- ❍ Have you got ants in your pants?
- ❍ The boys were hanging about in the corridor.

LIST 39

Misinterpretations by students

These comments are not fabrications but real examples of common phrases and their misinterpretations by young people on the autistic spectrum.

- It is not a level playing field. (Which playing field is he talking about?)
- It is like getting blood out of a stone. (You don't get blood out of a stone.)
- Hang on a minute. (Hang on to what?)
- Keep your hair on. (Why would I need to?)
- Don't keep me hanging on. (What are you going to hang on to?)
- Do I look stupid? (Well, actually, yes you do!)
- Do you think I was born yesterday? (You are not a baby so you can't have been.)
- Get a move on. (Where am I going?)
- Bull in a china shop. (How did it get there?)
- Save face. (Where do I keep it?)
- Don't overstep the mark. (Where is the mark?)

Students on the autistic spectrum might take all these literally.

- 'Give the pencils out' to them might mean literally 'give the pencils away for good'.
- If you say 'take a seat', they might wonder where they are supposed to take it.
- One boy, when asked what he wanted to do while it was raining cats and dogs, said 'Go inside so that they won't land on me'.
- The answer to 'Would you like to help me?' would probably be 'No'. They might help you but might not *like* to help you.

Using positive language

Recent research has highlighted the low level of language development that pupils have on entry to the education system. It has also shown that students in secondary schools often do not have the level of understanding or usage teachers think they have. It's essential therefore that you use clear and positive language in your classroom. Add your own to this list:

- ○ Nice try.
- ○ Very close.
- ○ Thanks for helping me.
- ○ You look smart today.
- ○ Your homework was good.
- ○ I know that is not true, so let's move on to something else.
- ○ That's arguing.
- ○ If you do what is asked then you get what you want.
- ○ If you listen you can have your whole breaktime.
- ○ Show me how well you can listen.
- ○ Show me eye contact.
- ○ Ryan, tell the others what I just said.
- ○ Ryan, how should we enter the classroom?
- ○ I am pleased that you settled quickly when you came into the classroom.

LIST 41   Reinforcing the message

It is possible to avoid some poor behaviour by using the right sort of language.

- Use non-verbal language to reinforce your behaviour, e.g. use your hand to make the 'stop' sign if the behaviour is unacceptable. Keep eye contact. Try to keep a straight face and do not let him or her see how you are feeling.
- Do not get into an argument or discussion. It is easy to be drawn into 'It's not fair! Darren did it first. Why pick on me?'
- Praise the behaviour rather than the student. Rather than saying, 'Good boy' or 'Good, Darren', it's more powerful to say, 'That was friendly behaviour towards Julie.'
- Use different tones of voice. If you use the same tone the students switch off to something you want them to pay attention to, so change your tone. Raise it and sound more forceful, without shouting.
- Remember, if you shout, they talk louder.
- If you notice a student is not doing the task correctly, don't say, 'No, you are doing it wrong, did you listen to a word I said?', but try, 'Why don't you draw a line there and copy the first line off the board here?'
- Stand near a student when giving instructions.
- Keep instructions short and precise, and make sure the first instruction is carried out before you move onto the next one.
- Ask the student to repeat the instructions back to you.
- Give students a table or list with an outline of key concepts and vocabulary to refer to.

Top tip: Always try to use positive language, even when commenting on poor behaviour.

Rewards and Sanctions

8

LIST 42   Views on reward systems

Rewards are a very powerful way to encourage students to do the 'right thing'. However, teachers, parents and pupils have different views – you'll be familiar with several of these.

- Why are the ones who misbehave rewarded as soon as they are good, when the majority of students are good all the time?
- Should students be rewarded for doing what they should be doing?
- Reward schemes may require a financial outlay, but surely students should want to learn for learning's sake!
- Different students respond to different rewards.
- Sanctions don't seem to be effective.
- I don't like the rewards we use in this school.
- Certificates are not worth the paper they are printed on.
- It takes too long to implement rewards.
- Parents told me off for suggesting that their child gets something extra on Friday night as a reward for hard work.
- I want to reward success, not effort.
- I want to reward effort, not just success.
- Rewards are too reminiscent of this materialistic society.
- Rewards are an American invention.
- They don't need these extensive reward systems in China.
- I haven't got time to sort out a system of rewards.

Despite some of these commonly held views, rewards are the most successful way we know of ensuring students behave, and they are much more effective than sanctions or punishments.

LIST 43 Using rewards

Research into using reward systems suggests that:

- tangible rewards, such as gifts, good marks, free time and visits tend to be very popular with the majority of students
- more boys than girls regard praise as effective
- more girls than boys regard marks as more effective
- boys and girls tend to agree that certificates and extra time are effective rewards
- few students believe that verbal warnings are very effective
- a letter or phone call home, extra work and detentions are regarded as effective by boys and girls
- the success of whole-school reward systems is totally dependent on how they are designed and how they are put into operation.

So, when considering rewards:

- use the system which pervades your school, and which should be laid out clearly in policy documents
- make sure your class is aware of the reward system and, if not, discuss it with them
- if you're considering introducing your own reward system, you must discuss it with your class and ensure that they fully understand it
- decide whether you favour tangible rewards or valued certificates
- find out if your students are better motivated by individual written or verbal feedback
- remember that the more effective you become as a teacher, the less reliant you will need to be on a formal system of rewards and sanctions.

LIST 44 Positive personal rewards

- A smile from you – you may not realize how powerful this really can be.
- Positive comments in an exercise book or folder.
- Some eye contact and appropriate facial expression implying thanks or praise.
- Verbal praise – when did someone last say 'well done' to you? Praise is a precious commodity and you can rarely overdo it, but only use it if the student has deserved it.
- A few moments or minutes of quality time from you. This can be a real booster, especially for those with a low self-image.
- Listening to a student. Some students rarely receive such treatment, but all will benefit and it will act as a good model for them.
- Showing an interest in their work, life or interests outside school.
- Playing games with students, in or out of class.
- Ensuring that peers give praise in some form. In certain circumstances an ovation may be called for.
- Giving praise in a written form to a high status person such as a head of department/house/year. Make sure they give feedback.

Different reward systems

○ Stickers and stars – these work well with younger groups. Let them save them up to get a tangible reward.

○ A merit or points system. Consider individual and group systems. The latter may utilize peer pressure.

○ A special class reward only given out by the teacher – focus in on student fads, such as a mouse mat with everyone's favourite film or cartoon character on it.

○ A headteacher's reward or a positive visit to a head of house/year or a favourite teacher.

○ Material rewards, e.g. sweets or fruit.

○ A best-effort award each week.

○ An automatic reward, especially for good behaviour – everyone who meets this target qualifies.

○ Certificates for whatever you choose – these are easy to produce on computers these days.

○ Trophies – these are easily obtained and cheapish if you don't go for a replica of the World Cup.

○ Recognition of behaviour at an assembly or other school gathering – this is not always utilized as often as it might be.

○ An award at presentation events.

Other effective rewards

- A standard positive letter or postcard which is sent to parents.
- An orange-juice party to be held at the end of the lesson, following a successful period of time.
- A food party where each student brings one item of food – remember to discuss religious differences.
- Top-up cards for mobile phones.
- Five minutes of talk time at the end of class.
- Supervised extra time on the sports field.
- Being first in a queue – this is always a real perk.
- Time to read a magazine, book or other material of choice for the last five minutes of a lesson (the amount of time should be agreed in advance).
- Listening to their choice of music (make sure you can tolerate the choice!).
- The chance to work with a friend on an activity instead of working alone.
- Access to a computer or MP3 player using a system where students collect cards or points – this encourages them to behave over a period of time.
- A display of work in the class, with names clearly and obviously mentioned – make sure other high status people comment in earshot of the student.
- Special privileges for an individual or group, such as using a special piece of equipment.
- Special jobs that are enjoyed or enhance status – perhaps taking the register, going on an errand, getting out special apparatus, handing out books.

Some of these may interfere with other teachers, so don't forget to inform them.

LIST 47 Sanctions: pros and cons

Sanctions tend to be less effective than rewards but are needed from time to time. There are advantages and disadvantages to every commonly used sanction (some call them punishments, but it's best not to use such negative language in our modern world). Examples include:

○ Detention – usually acceptable to teachers and students, does not usually interfere with work and many feel that this is an appropriate punishment. However, any delay in punishment reduces its effectiveness, and a detention is highly dependent on the pupil turning up. It also does not necessarily encourage a good attitude to work.

○ Verbal reprimand – this is quick and acceptable to many students, but it may make some react angrily, your class atmosphere may be spoiled, and it may make the situation worse.

○ Placing a student outside the classroom – this will certainly allow a cooling-off period but the student may miss work and may well misbehave outside.

○ Sending the student to a senior teacher – this does remove the problem from your class, but make sure that a senior teacher is available. Some people feel that such tactics demonstrate a weakness, although this is not the case if it forms part of school policy. Sending the pupil to another class is a possibility, but they may disrupt that class as well. The student may also enjoy the attention.

○ Giving lines – this may build up a negative attitude to work.

○ Phoning or contacting the parents – this can help to solve a problem, but remember you may not be able to contact them, or the parent may take the student's side and may not cooperate.

○ School reports – these often help to improve behaviour, involving the parents in monitoring the behaviour of the pupil. However, the report can be accidentally or deliberately lost.

Research suggests that students consider after-school detentions, a letter home to parents or a phone call to parents to be major penalties and these are most likely to improve their effort in terms of work and behaviour.

Using sanctions

You could consider using some of these sanctions:

- Ignore the behaviour – ensure that the student knows you are ignoring but not taking action (yet).
- Intervene non-verbally with a glance or a 'look'.
- Reprimand verbally – keep it brief and accurate, criticizing only the behaviour.
- Remind the student in a private place about the rules, how they have been violated and what behaviour is expected.
- Remind the student in a public place, but be careful as this can easily backfire and lead to greater problems.
- Register your disapproval through body language – this can be powerful.
- Ask for an apology – apologizing can be hard, as everyone knows.
- Use peer pressure – disapproval from peers is devastating, but be careful as it can work against you.
- Target the individual behaviour using your knowledge of the student and put some highly structured reward system in place.
- Devise a contract. These should have give and take clauses for you and the student. It is not good enough to say 'we will educate you if you behave'. In extreme cases the student doesn't want to come to school anyway, so what is in it for them?
- Make the student pay back lost time – this is always a good one, but a few minutes at breaktime is often enough, so don't punish yourself.
- Send the student to the headteacher.

LIST 49   **Effective sanctions**

- Deduct points or merits – although some would argue that you should never take away what has been earned.
- Give the student jobs around the school.
- Take away privileges – it's worth making a little list of these enjoyed by different students in each age group.
- Deny or limit access to a facility such as the school tuck-shop or a preferred leisure area.
- Exclude from breaktime or lunchtime. Remember, a late break or lunch can ruin the playground social life, so don't give up your entire break when ten minutes will severely affect theirs!
- Use report books or cards. Devise your own, possibly in conjunction with the pastoral staff if a school system is not in place.
- Discuss the offending behaviour with parents.
- Isolate the student from the class or group – decide for how long, and remember the sooner they come back, the sooner you can use the same sanction again if they still don't behave.
- Get a senior member of staff to remove the student. This is usually included in a school policy with a system for using it effectively.
- Use school sanctions, such as short-term exclusion – these often solve very little but may allow space for appropriate programmes to be devised.

Following up at the end of a lesson

If you have asked a student to stay for a while at the end of a lesson this is not the time for a diatribe. It is a time to:

- teach the broken rule
- administer the consequences
- suggest what should happen in future
- perhaps explain why the rule exists
- build a relationship
- try to leave on good terms.

Also remember to:

- thank the student for staying back
- check how they are feeling – if they are angry don't consider holding them back for more than a short while
- focus on the behaviour of concern, not the myriad of issues you are concerned about. This helps them learn about appropriate behaviour
- avoid the word 'you' as it can be intimidating, but certainly use 'I' in terms of feelings and expectations
- use the word 'when' – they probably don't break the rule every time
- ask for their comments
- get them to think about what they might do differently next time
- talk about personal responsibility but try to leave on an amicable note.

LIST 51 Detention

The 1997 Education Act gives schools legal backing to detain pupils after the end of a school session, so detention is certainly an available sanction. Here are some general points:

○ Detention can take place at lunchtime or after school – just when you want to be free.

○ Before it is used, pupils, parents and staff must be made aware that detention will be used as a sanction at school.

○ The 1997 Act states that schools must give at least 24 hours' written notice to the parents of the student concerned and this should happen before detention takes place after school hours.

○ Punishment is most effective when it immediately follows 'the crime' – the legally imposed time lag can almost nullify the effect of detention.

○ Parents of pupils who have started at the school through late admission must be made fully aware of the use of detention.

○ One study showed that the most common reason for being given detention was because the student had failed to attend detention. Make sure this is not the case for your students.

○ Students should be reminded on the day about detentions – this reduces the excuses for not attending and ensures that the more forgetful don't end up being excluded because of their poor memory.

○ Sitting doing nothing can lead to further difficulties. A constructive task will reduce problems and may even develop new personal or social skills.

Top tip: Good teaching is the best solution; reward systems work and sanctions are less effective.

Working with Others | 9

LIST 52 — Non-teaching staff

It is very important that all staff in schools work together to ensure good behaviour throughout the school. All schools have staff who are not directly teaching children, but do have regular contact with students. These include:

- office staff
- midday supervisors
- kitchen staff
- parents who come in to help
- the caretaker
- staff who work in the before- or after-school clubs.

It is vital that everyone:

- is aware of the policies and principles upon which the school operates
- appreciates that systems are only as strong as the weakest link
- realizes that students are very quick to work out who is a 'soft touch' when it comes to rule-breaking.

L I S T 53   Teaching assistants

Teaching assistants are now commonplace in the classroom. When they are in your class it is your role to manage them, although they will have their own duties to fulfil. Try to involve them as they will play an important part in ensuring good class behaviour.

Involve them where possible in:

- lesson and curriculum planning
- understanding the purpose and aims of the lesson
- preparing and collecting the required resources
- deciding their role in your classroom management
- greeting pupils on entry
- checking that pupils have the correct equipment
- checking that homework is completed
- using non-verbal cues to remind pupils of expected behaviours
- reminding pupils of the class rules
- supervising the tidying away of resources
- standing by the door to say goodbye to pupils
- checking that the room is ready for the next session.

Most importantly, if you ask for the attention of the class the teaching assistant should also attend, modelling the required good behaviour. This is essential for good class behaviour.

In other words, ensure that they contribute to the smooth running of your class.

LIST 54 The SENCO's role

In school the special educational needs coordinator (SENCO) has a crucial and pivotal role, especially when it comes to managing behaviour. This teacher takes responsibility for:

- overseeing the day-to-day operation of the school's SEN policy
- coordinating provision for the children with special educational needs
- liaising with and advising fellow teachers
- managing the learning support assistants
- overseeing the records of all children with special educational needs
- liaising with parents of children with special educational needs
- contributing to the in-service training of staff
- liaising with external agencies, including the local authority's support and educational psychology services, health and social services, and voluntary bodies.

To do this the SENCO must:

- have a clear understanding of SEN issues
- possess good organizational skills and high levels of knowledge in all areas of the curriculum and behaviour management
- be a human resource manager
- be able to manage budgets and identify areas of need
- actively support the needs of children and staff working in the school
- be able to work effectively with the senior management team, governors, parents and other agencies who visit school
- be highly knowledgeable with regards to legislation, subject information, the DfES guidance and guidance from other organizations
- write policies and reviews
- be able to assess pupils' individual needs and prepare appropriate programmes
- take responsibility for reviewing and monitoring progress.

LIST 55   Individual education plans

Children who have behavioural difficulties require their own individual education plan (IEP). These are prepared with the teachers and should:

○ identify the concerning behaviours
○ put appropriate strategies into place
○ be discussed with parents and the student
○ contain targets which are SMART:
  – Specific
  – Measurable
  – Attainable
  – Relevant
  – Time-related
○ be supported by work in the classroom and in the whole school
○ be made known to all members of staff in contact with the student
○ be kept under continual review and evaluated at least twice a year.

The SENCO may have briefing sessions to keep staff informed, and outside agencies may be involved with supporting the student and providing information. Sometimes additional support, from within the school's resources, is allocated to the student.

L I S T 5 6   What an IEP contains

Pupils with special problems will have an individual education plan (IEP). This may look at how behavioural issues should be addressed by all staff, though there may be subject-specific references. It is important for you and the pupil that you follow the plans set out in the IEP.

The IEP itself should include information about:

○ the short-term targets set for or by the student
○ the teaching strategies to be used to meet these targets
○ the provision which has to be put into place
○ the review date
○ the success and/or exit criteria
○ the actual outcomes (to be recorded when the IEP is reviewed)
○ information that is additional to or different from the differentiated curriculum plan.

With behaviour this will mean you:

○ must implement the procedures indicated
○ should not use your own preferred interventions instead
○ must be consistent in this implementation
○ keep a note of any problems or successes
○ report to the SENCO or head of department any successes, failures or problems so that the IEP can be refined or subject-specific issues can be taken into account.

Top tip: There are others there to help you.

More Challenging Behaviour

10

LIST 57 Dealing with confrontation

If at all possible, confrontation should be avoided. However, sometimes it is inevitable so here are some points to remember.

○ Only get involved if you feel you can handle it and you have sufficient support.

○ Seek help immediately if you know it is going to be a difficult situation.

○ Send a student for another pertinent member of staff and make sure you choose a student who is reliable.

○ Remember to be critical of the behaviour, not the person.

○ Be seen to be in control and apparently containing the situation. This may not always be the reality but it is important to look as though it is.

○ Use your authority. This is your greatest strength and is recognized by all students. Use the name of the student as this is a way of attracting attention and indicating power.

○ Set limits for the student. Comments such as, 'You have two minutes to stop this, come downstairs and we will talk,' give you something to say, set limits and give an instruction. Remember that difficult confrontations mean that the student has lost control of their behaviour and they need time to calm down a little.

L I S T 58 Coping with your emotions

○ If you feel angry enough to hit the student or assault them in any way, you must walk away from the situation. Stay in the vicinity to make sure that no one is injured but ensure that other help is called.

○ As soon as the confrontation has finished, get back to normal as quickly as possible. Do not mention the behaviour, do not mention past behaviour and do not talk about the confrontation until the student (and you) have fully calmed down. This may be hours later or even the next day.

○ Be aware of your own emotions. You are likely to feel a range of emotions, including anger, humiliation, a feeling that you have been deskilled or are unable to cope. This is normal for all of us and quite legitimate in extreme situations, but it is important that you don't let these emotions cloud your judgement.

○ Avoid negative or aggressive responses – although it takes courage to pull back from an emotional situation in a calm, controlled way, a negative reaction on your part models poor behaviour and may reinforce negative experiences the student has suffered.

○ If your mistake led to the confrontation, admit it. This in itself sets a very positive example of behaviour.

○ Most importantly, avoid all confrontational situations unless they are absolutely essential and may enable a student to move forward. Unnecessary confrontations are bad for your health!

L I S T 5 9 Tips for dealing with explosive situations

In very serious confrontations it is important to remember the following tips:

- Never patronize or talk down to the student.
- Ensure that you do not get cornered or, more importantly, corner the student.
- Do not make threats or ultimatums you cannot later enforce – this is tempting, especially in 'the heat of the moment'.
- Aim to achieve cooperation rather than confrontation, so use your authority and keep calm.
- Lower your voice as this helps to defuse the whole atmosphere and demonstrates your (apparent) control.
- Listen to what they have to say – you may have heard it all before but it's difficult for a student to tell their story and remain confrontational and angry at the same time. Persuading a student to talk can prove a very calming exercise.
- Reflect the anger by saying something like, 'I can see you're angry and I'd like you to tell me about it.'
- Back off from the situation, if this is appropriate – neither you nor the student should get hurt.
- Yield ground but keep talking in order to calm the situation.
- Consider standing at right angles to the student as this is a less confrontational pose.
- Maintain appropriate eye contact.
- Remove any audience if at all possible and always seek assistance.
- Try not to use physical contact in any way, but do so if there is a risk to a person.
- Avoid restraint unless you have been instructed to use it.
- Use the broken record technique. Keep repeating the same comment over and over again, 'If you calm down, I'll listen to you.' This at least gives you something to say.
- Remember, these situations are draining so try and find time for a short break afterwards. Talk to other staff to help you normalize yourself and the situation. Don't forget to do the same for others.

LIST 60   Avoiding permanent exclusion

Extremely difficult situations are rare in most schools but sometimes students cause so many problems in a school there is a real possibility that they will be permanently excluded. Such students may also be at risk of being involved in criminal activity. Under these circumstances a pastoral support programme (PSP) may be necessary and a school must provide one. A PSP:

- is school based
- is designed to help individuals manage their behaviour
- has a very definite structure which is transparent and precise
- has realistic outcomes
- is overseen by one member of staff
- is automatically set up after several fixed-period exclusions
- does not replace other assessment processes. These should continue or may be instigated as part of the plan
- does not replace an appropriately drawn up individual educational plan
- is designed to ensure continued education
- should not leave the pupil on the streets. A major aim is to cut crime
- must be agreed with parents, who must be kept regularly informed of progress
- must involve the local authority, which will agree how it will help and assist with monitoring
- requires a meeting of interested parties and agencies, such as social services, housing, voluntary or statutory agencies.

Joint efforts to avoid exclusion

Exclusion is of little use to pupil, school or potential school. In exceptional circumstances it may prove necessary, but it can reflect badly on a school. There is now at least one local authority that has managed a whole school year without one permanent exclusion from any of its schools. Every possible step should be taken to avoid such exclusion. Relevant school staff, the local support services and others working with the pupil should discuss all the issues and factors contributing to the problem. On the agenda for discussion could be:

○ a profile of the individual student in some depth
○ any learning difficulties the student may have
○ the literacy skills which may be inhibiting progress
○ a programme to address any or all of these as appropriate
○ whether to disapply from the National Curriculum – this is allowable under certain circumstances but should be resisted where possible as it can lead to further problems
○ potential issues (and solutions) in different curriculum areas
○ the student's grouping and seating arrangements
○ the use of any special facility within the school
○ a possible referral to a pupil referral unit (an off-site placement usually)
○ a move to another school
○ the possible need for specialist support – what, who and where
○ the need for a learning support unit at the school or off-site
○ any other constructive way forward.

Top tip: Avoid or remove audiences when dealing with difficult situations.

Bullying at School 11

LIST 62 What is bullying?

Students learn most effectively in schools where they and staff feel safe, secure and happy. This means we must all treat each other with kindness and respect. Bullying is where a student or a group of students exercise some kind of control over another against their will. All bullying behaviour has three things in common:

- it is deliberate and hurtful
- it is repeated a number of times (one-off situations are not usually regarded as bullying)
- it is difficult for those being bullied to defend themselves.

Bullying may involve:

- physical behaviour – hitting, kicking or stealing possessions
- verbal behaviour – name-calling, insults, racist remarks or even threats
- more indirect behaviour – such as spreading true or untrue stories about the victim or excluding them from groups.

LIST 63   Types of bullying

- Pushing, shoving, punching, kicking, poking
- Severe physical assault
- Abusive telephone calls – especially vicious when texted on a mobile phone
- Physical harassment or the infliction of pain
- Interference with a desk or even a pencil case
- Personal property defaced, broken, stolen or hidden
- Demands for money in or out of school
- Aggressive body language
- The 'look'
- Nasty notes – these can be frightening
- Sending to 'Coventry' or any other place for that matter
- Name-calling – slaphead, knob, queen, paki, prossie, fatty, baldy, teacher's pet, four eyes...
- Personal remarks about appearance, or personal hygiene
- Verbal abuse, threats to people's families, etc
- Damage to clothing or school books.

Make sure *you* do not bully by using:

- sarcasm
- humiliating methods
- degrading exercises
- intimidating gestures.

LIST 64   Why young people bully

Young people might bully because they:

- may live with people who abuse them in some way
- may have learnt that aggression and violence are effective
- believe dominating others is the best means to get their own way
- live in a household which is harsh and where physical punishment is common
- live for part of their life in an environment which is highly inconsistent in terms of its rewards and punishments
- have faced sudden emotional outbursts
- have not been taught it is wrong
- are encouraged to bully by friends
- believe it is just a 'bit of fun'
- believe this is how one socializes
- are going through a difficult time at home or school
- are copying behaviour they have seen
- have been a victim of bullying
- have a strong wish to dominate others
- have found their size and strength or even age are useful ways of achieving goals.

LIST 65   Understanding bullies and victims

Students regularly need to be made aware that bullying will not be tolerated in school. All staff should be vigilant, especially when on duty around the school environment.

Bullies:

○ are often popular and have a 'following' of students who like to be seen to be in the core group
○ rarely bully on their own if part of a group, preferring the presence of the main bully to enhance their confidence
○ place a lot of importance on power and status
○ regularly tell lies to get out of trouble
○ often blame others and show little remorse for their actions.

Victims:

○ are often passive loners who are targeted as they readily respond and have few self-defence skills
○ tend not to be able to retaliate quickly verbally and are particularly sensitive to the comments of others. They may have weak language skills which makes it more difficult to ignore or in any way deflect comment
○ may have special vulnerabilities, such as sensitivity about their lifestyle or family, the clothes they wear or their physical attributes
○ occasionally retaliate with little chance of 'winning'.

Research into bullying

Research indicates that the three most helpful factors in preventing bullying or helping pupils to deal with bullies are:

○ friendships
○ avoidance strategies
○ learning to 'stand up for yourself'.

Reporting bullying is associated with several risks, and children tend to fear that:

○ their confidentiality is likely to be breached
○ nothing will be done
○ they will not be protected from the future actions of bullies
○ their parents might not believe them or might overreact and make matters worse
○ their parents might worry too much.

Important sources of help include:

○ parents – for emotional support and advice and for raising concerns about bullying with teachers
○ confidential services, such as counselling services and voluntary organizations working with children and young people. Such organizations enable students to express their feelings, consider the options available to them, and have some control over the pace of disclosure should they decide to tell a teacher or parent about bullying.

Based on a report called *Tackling Bullying* by Christine Oliver and Mano Candappa (Thomas Coram Research Unit, Institute of Education, 2003).

L I S T 67   Taking action

If you think that a student is distressed because they are being bullied you must act quickly to avoid further damage to self-esteem or to their physical and mental well-being.

- ○ Read and follow the school policy on bullying.
- ○ Know the school code on behaviour and discipline and enforce it.
- ○ Keep your eyes open for possible bullying.
- ○ Always act as a good role model.
- ○ Develop good self-esteem in the bully and the victim.
- ○ Listen carefully to the victim and the bully.
- ○ Record incidents accurately.
- ○ Check out facts where you can.
- ○ Try not to blame young people.
- ○ Make it clear that the behaviour is unacceptable.
- ○ Discuss the general issue of how to behave with your class.
- ○ Get the victim and the bully to record the incident – this helps to demonstrate its seriousness.
- ○ Tell pupils to report any bullying or harassment and act on the information immediately.
- ○ Stress the horrendous nature of such behaviour to all.
- ○ Teach bullies how to behave appropriately.
- ○ Help victims to be less vulnerable to name-calling, and not to retaliate when bullied – remind them that others are called names as well and point out that most of the taunts are not true or valid ones.
- ○ Try to build self-esteem by talking about strengths rather than weaknesses.

Some anti-bullying strategies

Tackling bullying in school is essential and it is important that activities take place throughout the school which reduce the possibility of bullying and help pupils to find more acceptable ways of interacting with each other. The following activities and strategies could be helpful:

○ Set up social skills training sessions for more vulnerable students, especially those with language difficulties, those lacking verbal skills, or students on the autistic spectrum.

○ Give bullies the chance of making restitution (see the George Robinson and Barbara Maines *No Blame Approach* published by Lucky Duck Publishing).

○ Teach students strategies to use in situations where their peers are being bullied.

○ Teach students at risk of bullying strategies to avoid getting into situations likely to promote bullying.

○ Teach students at risk of bullying how to deal with certain situations, such as name-calling, and how to leave a threatening situation.

○ Reframe the behaviour of the bully by getting them to take on a position of responsibility and help them see the benefits of positive rather than negative behaviour towards others.

LIST 69
Peer-support and mentoring schemes

Pupil counsellors or peer-support schemes are popular to help reduce the amount of bullying in schools. They involve training the pupils to help create a safe and supportive environment for others.

The benefits

○ Pupils are able to talk about bullying and other peer-relationship issues on a confidential and individual basis.

○ Pupils often prefer to speak to someone in their year or someone who is slightly older, rather than to an adult. Adults, being so much older than the pupil, are perceived as being 'out of touch' with current situations.

○ Pupils can be helped with the transition from Year 6 to Year 7. Mentors play an important role, visiting feeder primary schools. The children in the primary school identify with the mentors and are able to spend time with them on entry to the senior school.

○ Peer supporters and mentors are trained to recognize those issues that they can deal with and those that need passing on to another person. They are taught listening, coping and negotiating skills, often by professional counsellors.

○ The young people, when trained, are empowered to help their peers find solutions to problems.

○ Both the mentor and the pupil benefit from the scheme.

Top tip: Be alert to small events that could potentially spark greater difficulties.

Dealing with Anger 12

What is anger?

Anger is:

- a natural, healthy, appropriate, life-enhancing emotion
- a great communicator, often the only one young people have to convey their distress
- often from our own past.

When you are dealing with anger it is important to remember that:

- the angry feelings students exhibit don't mean they're 'bad' and these feelings need not be frightening to parents or professionals
- it is far better that the anger is shown and students learn to deal with it rather than 'bottling it up' inside
- some people can take a lot of criticism or anger and are difficult to arouse, while others will 'blow up' at the slightest thing – 'He touched me, Miss'
- being angry means students are usually emotionally involved, possibly out of control, and may feel ashamed or incompetent.

LIST 71   Managing anger

It is not always possible to avoid situations or people, or to leave the environment that makes you angry, so you have to learn to control your emotions and subsequent reactions. There are many approaches to managing anger, three of which are expressing, suppressing and calming.

- Expressing anger – this can be done in an assertive way rather than an aggressive way. Students have to learn to make clear what their needs are and how they can be met.
- Suppressing anger – the anger should be suppressed and converted into more constructive behaviour. However, anger does need an outward expression as internalization can create physical or mental problems.
- Calming anger – students need to control their inward anger. Techniques include counting to ten and popping bubble wrap.

It is also useful to remember that:

- some students have low anger thresholds
- not all students have had the opportunity to develop control techniques within their family
- students brought up in a family situation which lacks structure and with few opportunities to learn the skill of communicating their feelings will have problems in managing their own anger
- negative language rarely reflects reality.

So:

- Students need to know we all have bad days. Talk about your own bad days and how you retrieved positives from negatives.
- Emphasize the need to 'think before you speak', especially when angry.
- Talk through difficult situations with students.
- Encourage students to laugh at difficult situations – defusing situations with humour can be very useful.

LIST 72 Helping others control aggression

Here are some suggestions for young people to help them manage their anger and control their aggression.

- Walk away from the situation.
- Count to ten slowly.
- Be aware of the situation and try and avoid being part of it.
- Consider the consequences before reacting.
- Change your thinking about the situation – this will need discussion with the teacher.
- Practise slow breathing.
- Distract yourself by thinking or doing something else.
- Cultivate a sense of humour.
- Ask yourself 'is it really important?'
- Practise assertiveness.
- Empathize with the other person.
- Maintain sensible eye contact.
- Don't interrupt angry people.

LIST 73 An anti-aggression exercise

If you are a form teacher, try this useful exercise to find out what makes the individuals in your class angry.

- Give each student a piece of paper.
- Ask them to write down three things that make them angry in class.
- Ask them to fold these and place them in a box.
- Then get an attentive student to select a piece of paper and read it out.
- With a show of hands, ask the other students to vote 'yes' or 'no' to this comment.
- Record on paper or on the board the comment and the number of affirmatives.
- Choose another good role model to pick another piece of paper to read out.
- Repeat the procedure.
- Over a number of weeks spend a few sessions doing this until the majority of comments have been voted on.
- At the next session, give one of these examples and ask for suggestions on how to deal with it.
- Get the students to write down their suggestions and put them in the box.
- Ask a student to read out a suggestion.
- As before, students vote on the suggestion.
- Spend time going through as many strategies as possible.
- Ask students to draw a poster, each using a 'speech bubble' for a scenario likely to anger someone in class.
- Get the students to write or draw strategies to deal with each scenario.

L I S T 74   **Things to avoid**

When dealing with angry people, never:

- ○ fold your arms – it creates a barrier between you and them
- ○ stand too close – it invades their space and feels confrontational
- ○ wag your finger – it's intimidating and winds people up
- ○ use any other explicit or rude gesture
- ○ tower over people – this suggests power or control and is almost bullying-type behaviour
- ○ humiliate – this often has repercussions at a later date
- ○ keep the anger going – this is not constructive in any way
- ○ make any physical contact, even of the gentlest nature – this could be interpreted incorrectly and lead to more difficulties (even guiding a pupil may lead to disaster)
- ○ raise your voice – try to sound calm and consciously lower your voice
- ○ ignore them – this can lead to even more ferocity
- ○ interrupt them – they will just shout or scream louder
- ○ laugh – they want to be taken seriously
- ○ look disinterested – this situation is foremost in their minds
- ○ talk about past misdemeanours
- ○ smile – it irritates them even more
- ○ challenge them until after the anger has subsided, and even then be as circumspect as you possibly can. The challenge may bring back the anger and therefore the difficult situation.

Using role-play

A good technique for managing anger is to use role-play and script possible future scenarios.

○ Identify a particular problem situation with a student. This may require much discussion, but try to find a situation that the student finds especially difficult and is motivated to do something about.

○ Work out the needs of the other party, preferably with the student who gets angry. This in itself is a useful exercise as it helps the student understand that there is more than one perspective on any social situation.

○ Define the student's own needs. For example, he or she may want to join in a particular game but for some reason is not allowed to do so. Explore the reasons, but define exactly what the student wants. There may be an alternative game that they can join in with.

○ Try to devise a 'win–win' situation. Playing a game with another group, for example, would allow the student to win and the group that doesn't want the student also wins!

○ Talk through what the other party might say or do. This is likely to be based on the immediate past unpleasant experiences of the student but turn it into a discussion about consequences if different actions are taken.

○ Now talk through what your student might say or do when faced by the situation that causes distress.

○ Practise this using role-play. You don't have to hold an Equity card to do this! You will need to run through the scenario a number of times. The more you practise the greater the chance it will be used in a real situation.

○ Seek feedback on its success and don't forget to praise the student.

○ If the script did not work, re-evaluate it with the student and instigate changes to it to cope with any unforeseen variables – neither of you has the crystal ball to see everything!

L I S T 7 6   An anger-management exercise

Use this for yourself, your pupils or your colleagues.

○ Tense your muscles and breathe in.
○ Stay tense for five seconds.
○ Now begin to relax, starting with your head and moving slowly down to your feet – breathing out slowly as you do this.
○ Repeat the above several times.
○ Once you can do this, think of someone who has made you angry or something that has frustrated you.
○ Tense up, focus on your anger or frustration.
○ Relax, as indicated above.
○ As you relax, feel the anger draining out of you.
○ Feel the emotion leaking out of the tips of your toes and visualize it as a puddle at your feet.
○ Once you have drained your anger, step away from the puddle and leave your anger behind.

Top tip: Whatever your mood, look calm, cool and collected, even if you don't feel it.

Special Problems 13

LIST 77 — Students with additional needs

It is very likely that you will have some young people in your class with very special problems. Hopefully you will have been alerted to these and will have received advice from others, including the special needs department. Such advice is important and clearly must be followed.

These behaviours may be seen in varying degrees in some of the young people you teach:

○ low self-esteem
○ restless mind
○ restlessness
○ poor time management
○ impatience and frustration
○ poor social skills, together with the making of inappropriate remarks
○ feelings of underachievement
○ concentration problems
○ forgetfulness and poor short-term memory
○ lack of organization
○ problems with creating and maintaining routines
○ lack of self-discipline
○ impulsive behaviour.

These are the types of behaviours on checklists for the diagnosis of attention deficit hyperactivity disorder (ADHD) but they can also be seen in other conditions and many children may present them from time to time. It is important to note that before a student is diagnosed as having ADHD, other factors have to be taken into consideration and ideally a multidisciplinary assessment is carried out, with the final diagnosis resting with a consultant child and adolescent psychiatrist or paediatrician.

LIST 78 Helping dyspraxic students

Dyspraxia is defined as motor difficulties caused by perceptual problems, especially visual-motor and kinaesthetic-motor difficulties. Dyspraxic students are poorly organized and are likely to have quite severe coordination difficulties which can cause problems in the classroom in terms of relationships with others, lack of success and so on. Implementing appropriate strategies can reduce stress for the student, stress for yourself and improve behaviour in lessons.

○ Colour-code the student's timetable.
○ Laminate a short list of equipment needed for each school day.
○ If concentration is an issue, frequently cue the pupil in by name during lessons, e.g. 'George, look at page 24 and tell me...'
○ Be tolerant – broken and lost equipment is par for the course for people with dyspraxia!
○ In science, consider the extra and enhanced hazards for a clumsy person. Pair them with a well-coordinated student for lab work. Praise them for knowledge of theory, avoiding criticism of organization for practical experiments.
○ Graphs and maps will prove difficult, and organizing a visual display of any kind will be a problem, so provide more careful explanation, patience and understanding.
○ Teach the whole class as though they had organization difficulties. Use a step-by-step guided approach, 'First get out...then put...' Demonstrate or use visual aids.
○ Drawing is another problematic area, but is often improved if you can provide an object to copy.
○ Technology lessons can be 'an accident waiting to happen'. Set a task which uses larger pieces of material for construction rather than 'fiddly' little pieces.
○ If you teach PE then encourage the less well-coordinated students to beat their personal best records rather than try to compete on a playing field which is not level!
○ Don't insist that the dyspraxic student joins a team of well-coordinated students as this only causes resentment on the part of the coordinated group and embarrassment on the part of the dyspraxic. Differentiate by setting an alternative activity which has a success element built in to enable the student to 'save face'.

- Help them to develop those gross motor skills which they struggle with.
- Use large balls for catching rather than small balls.
- Use large bats and racquets.
- Use up-turned benches for walking along to improve balance.

LIST 79   Understanding autism

Imagine you know nothing about the feelings of others or how to interpret facial expressions or understand double entendres and satire. You have put yourself in the 'shoes' of someone on the autistic spectrum. You can quickly understand how behaviour problems can arise.

Life can be very confusing for someone with an autistic spectrum disorder (ASD). They have to interpret our intentions without many of the clues or cues which we take for granted. They may be asked to do something and then criticized for not doing what was asked. So,

- Be specific in what it is you require – a literal interpretation of your homework question can result in a poor mark and increased anxiety for the student.
- Try not to take offence if a 'blunt' remark is made by the student with ASD about some aspect of your physical features.
- Remember, the learning of rules of social conduct and of appropriate remarks to make takes some time.
- Think of the analogy of a computer with limited software. A program needs writing and inputting to get the required results from the computer. Staff need to work on teaching those aspects of social skills which are not yet learnt.

Coping with ADHD

With students who have special educational needs which affect their behaviour in class, such as ADHD, it is important to remember that the condition is not the student's fault. Yes, they can control some of the behaviour, but for the majority of time they cannot. So,

❍ Don't get into punishment mode and give detentions. This does not help the student change their behaviour but can lead them into greater problems which may create even more stress for you – so develop ways of dealing with it.

❍ Some ADHD students are reported to 'get on with' some teachers better than others. Ask those teachers how they deal with the behaviour. If they say that the behaviour does not occur in their lessons, then ask about the lesson in terms of content, management style, language, seating positions, etc.

❍ Try to emulate that environment in your lessons, even if it means changing your style of teaching for that lesson and putting in some extra effort. The ADHD student is not deliberately trying to be awkward, even if it appears to be the case. Remember, you are the adult. Try to lessen the chances of confrontation. Change conditions so that there is no antecedent.

❍ Remember, the ADHD student has a need for stimulation. In some cases it is treated using medication and this itself can create management problems, such as the need to receive the medication at specific times. Ritalin is often used and is a short-acting drug, unless the student is on a slow-release tablet.

Some of the above behaviours can also be seen in students who have dyspraxia, among other difficulties (see List 78 Helping dyspraxic students).

Simple teaching tips

For those with attention issues some extra individual support should prove helpful.

○ Provide students with a 'stress ball' or even Blu-Tack or Plasticine to fiddle with.
○ Try to report only positive comments in any home–school diary.
○ Give some kind of position of responsibility to the student, with a simple checklist as an aide memoire.
○ Provide written lists and outlines which follow your class instructions – these can be used with any students who have special educational needs but are particularly useful for ADHD students who may be seen talking in class, asking others what to do.
○ Use a recognizable signal to gain attention, e.g. raising your hand or snapping your fingers.
○ Use frequent eye contact so that the student knows that you are 'engaging' them.
○ Reinforce positive behaviour, e.g. as soon as the student makes a start on his/her work, approach them and quietly acknowledge this. Also make sure that they continue working!
○ Make lists of key vocabulary for use with ADHD and other students.
○ Time management is a problem for ADHD students, so help them plan a project and divide it into chunks to be completed within set time limits.
○ Encourage the ADHD student to attend a homework club. This structured environment promotes completion of a task, and adult support is present should the student require it.
○ Consider strategies which bypass the difficult behaviour, such as encouraging the student to change activity.

LIST 82   Organizing the learning environment

For virtually every individual problem you will need to provide a structured learning environment, and the following points could be considered.

○ Manage any medical needs, from medicine to crutches.
○ Provide consistent methods and routines.
○ Try to ensure that there is a high degree of predictability within lessons.
○ If students need to learn specialist skills, ensure that someone is available to help them.
○ Think about your seating plan. The ADHD student should not be looking out of the window and the highly dyspraxic student should not be near apparatus that could easily be knocked over!
○ Position students so that they have good access to appropriate role models – students can learn a lot from their peers.
○ Try to avoid distractions within the classroom.
○ Avoid unpredictable transitions wherever possible.
○ Provide a quiet area in the classroom, where stimuli are reduced.
○ Remember, staff and pupils need to be involved and will need to work together.

LIST 83 Modifying your requirements

If a student is having difficulty coping with work, you can modify what it is you require them to do. Try to:

○ encourage the student to seek assistance regularly during the lesson
○ make your directions clear and concise, perhaps asking the student to repeat them to ensure that they have heard and understood
○ simplify complex directions wherever possible
○ gradually reduce assistance as they start to cope more adequately
○ consider a daily assignment notebook – this helps alleviate your workload – and, if possible, use a buddy to help them to work through your demands
○ make sure that there is plenty of time for the student to write down homework or provide them with a photocopied sheet
○ keep the student involved for as much of the time as possible
○ present material in small chunks. Students can cope more easily with small amounts of material. This means you can monitor their work more satisfactorily as well
○ give additional time to students for all tasks. Many students with special needs require extra time to undertake tasks and if you are not careful it is you who gives up break to allow them to finish the unrealistic amount of set work!

LIST 84 Assigning tasks

When giving tasks and assessing performance remember that those with behavioural difficulties will struggle if they have too much on their plate. So:

○ Try to give only one task at a time. Any hint of multi-tasking will be counter-productive in that little if anything will get done.

○ Monitor the student with difficulties frequently. This ensures that they keep on task, and if they don't, appropriate action can be taken immediately.

○ Modify all assignments as needed. Differentiation is now commonplace but it really is essential for these students, so give special thought to them.

○ Ensure that you test the knowledge of the student and not how long they are attending to the task you are giving. Too often those with a behaviour problem lose interest in or concentration on the task at hand and any assessment is merely investigating this rather than their knowledge or skills.

○ Try to ensure that problematic students do not become frustrated. Frustration is a major cause of the more severe forms of challenging behaviour. Work that is too easy or too difficult or very boring can cause real difficulty. Monitoring the student can help avoid this.

○ If you have a particularly difficult student, consider sending them on an errand. This allows you to settle the rest of the class and you can give the difficult student more attention when they re-enter your classroom.

○ Organize errands with other colleagues.

○ Consider a cueing system for colleagues. A simple system, such as taking a note with an obscure message to a colleague, can cue them into holding on to a pupil for five minutes or so while you settle the class.

LIST 85   Enhancing self-esteem

Poor self-esteem leads to poor self-confidence which tends to produce poor behaviour. When dealing with an individual who needs a word:

○ use covert communication – discuss any issues with the student in private. This is sometimes called 'conferencing'

○ give constructive feedback – don't just tell students off, explain what they need to do next time. Be constructive and positive in the discussion

○ establish consequences – ensure that students are fully aware of the potential consequences of their actions. They may not have grasped fully the implications of their actions and the rules

○ administer consequences – this is particularly important for learning

○ avoid using ridicule and criticism – such actions are remembered for the rest of the student's life. Do you really want to be remembered posthumously in this way?

LIST 86 Behaviour contracts

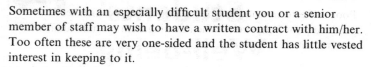

Sometimes with an especially difficult student you or a senior member of staff may wish to have a written contract with him/her. Too often these are very one-sided and the student has little vested interest in keeping to it.

The contract should:

○ specify the behaviours seen as a problem
○ require both sides to work together towards a solution
○ state clearly and concisely the plan to be followed by both parties
○ involve both teacher(s) and student in its composition. If necessary a learning mentor could help the student to write their contribution
○ be of some benefit to all involved
○ use positive terms and rewards rather than the threat of sanctions
○ set criteria such as three out of five successful outcomes to ensure that the student does not 'give up' at the first situation they cannot handle
○ be formally typed up and perhaps witnessed by parents or others to give it even more status.

Be prepared to renegotiate the terms in the event of failure.

Top tip: For those special children, seek advice and read the paperwork.

Managing Students' Well-being 14

 Planning school trips

School trips are fun but supply many jokes about the behaviour of students, and unfortunately it is often the teacher who is the butt. Make sure you read your school policy on school trips and consult your local authority or government guidelines before undertaking the trip.

- Prepare a procedure for what to do if a student gets lost or separated from the main group and explain it to the students.
- Pair the student with another one (friends if possible) – emphasize the responsibility for looking out for each other.
- Compile a list of student mobile phone numbers in case they are separated from the main party.
- Explain sanctions for bringing the school into disrepute and give examples of unacceptable behaviour.
- Print out some guidelines of how to enjoy a trip rather than a list of what not to do.
- In PSHE, highlight and talk about a person's right to privacy.
- Discuss what students should do if they discover personal facts about others in the class or about a member of staff. Get students to think of some examples and how they would react. Role-play potential situations but handle this sensitively.
- Get students to list their possessions.
- Ask them to check periodically against this list, e.g. at the end or beginning of each day.
- Ensure that information divulged on individual student consent forms is kept confidential, and reassure parents that this is the case. More information is likely to be given by parents if they feel that confidentiality will not be breached. Staff have to ensure a

student's health and welfare is not discussed within hearing distance of another student. Enquire about allergies, food sensitivities, phobias, medical regimes, etc.

○ Set some time aside, perhaps after the evening meal, for students to seek individual advice, e.g. about home sickness, having no friends, personal problems, an accident – this is applicable to boys as well as girls.

○ Handle personal student information sensitively. A few young people suffer from enuresis (bedwetting). Parents do not always notify staff of this as students worry that they won't be allowed to go or that other students will laugh at them. Dyspraxia and emotional problems can be possible causes of enuresis, and boys as old as 15 can suffer from this, especially when in an unfamiliar environment.

LIST 88   Medical needs on school trips

Virtually every school trip will have students with some medical issues which will need monitoring or medicating. Students cannot be expected to take full responsibility for this, especially when they have been highly reliant on their parents. Behaviour issues will arise over what otherwise might be a trivial matter if students do not believe or feel that these needs are being met.

- Explain to students who to go to with medical problems (such as blisters, travel sickness) or female problems (emergency supplies, etc).
- Make a list of who suffers from travel sickness and ensure that they have taken medication (with parental permission). Sit the student near the front of the coach/minibus and have sick bags at the ready, just in case.
- Be prepared to support adolescent girls who are menstruating – when away from home they often need some reassurance that it is not 'the end of the world' or an embarrassment if they have an accident.
- Assign epileptics, diabetics or those with other conditions which require daily medication to a member of staff who can supervise them. Ensure that you have a member of staff trained to administer medication (epipens, etc) in an emergency and that you know who to contact. Staff should be extra vigilant regarding the physical limitations of such students. Prior to leaving home, written parental consent should be obtained by the school. Up-to-date professional union clarification regarding these matters should be sought.
- If Ritalin is required by any student, make sure a designated adult stores it in a safe and secure place as it is a classified drug.
- Remember, any student with an allergy will require adult supervision. Asthmatics are at greater risk in summer away from their normal environment and when subjected to new foods/allergens. For severe reactions, such as anaphylactic shock, a student may need to carry an epipen.
- Take a fully charged mobile phone.
- Give a card listing parental contact numbers to each staff member.
- A trained first-aider should be available and known to all.

Child protection

School staff have a duty of care to each other and to all students. They should be aware of the school's:

○ health and safety policy
○ emergency procedures
○ accident and security procedures
○ areas of risk
○ other policies, e.g. first-aid, medication.

Also, local authorities and governing bodies must:

○ make arrangements to ensure that their duties are fulfilled with regard to safeguarding and promoting the welfare of children
○ have regard for any government guidance issued.

Where there are concerns about children and young people's welfare, all agencies must take all appropriate actions to address those concerns, working to agreed local policies and procedures. The Children Act 2004 puts a duty on almost everyone to do this and this Act underpins the Government's Every Child Matters agenda, now being implemented nationwide.

Through their day-to-day contact with pupils, and direct work with families, education staff have a crucial role to play in noticing indicators of possible abuse or neglect, and in referring concerns to the senior designated teacher – make sure you know who this is in your school.

The senior designated teacher:

○ is responsible for coordinating action on child protection
○ liaises with other agencies about child protection concerns and referrals
○ offers support and advice to staff who may have concerns about pupils in school.

L I S T 90   Types of abuse

Abuse is when a child is hurt or harmed by another person in a way that causes significant harm to that child and which may well have an effect on the child's development or well-being.

○ Physical abuse – may involve hitting, throwing, poisoning, burning or scalding, drowning, suffocating, or otherwise causing physical harm to a child. Physical harm may also be caused when a parent or carer feigns the symptoms of or deliberately causes ill health in a child they are looking after.

○ Emotional abuse – actual or likely adverse effect on the emotional and behavioural development of a child under the age of 18 years, caused by persistent or severe emotional ill-treatment or rejection.

○ Neglect – persistent or severe neglect of children under the age of 18 years, or the failure to protect a child from exposure to any kind of danger.

○ Sexual abuse – the actual or likely sexual exploitation of a child or adolescent under the age of 18 by any person. This includes any form of sexual activity to which the young person cannot give true consent either by law or because of ignorance, dependence, development, immaturity or fear.

LIST 91

Golden rules in abuse cases

Child abuse is a minefield and much damage can be done unintentionally by concerned adults. Any evidence that the adult may have in any way led the child or suggested words to the child could leave the child vulnerable as no action can be taken. Worse still, serious abusers will have to be let off by the courts and allowed to abuse elsewhere.

○ Make sure you read your school policy and know the designated teacher to contact.

○ Listen carefully to what the young person has to say, but do not question them in a way that puts words in their mouth.

○ When listening, try to say nothing or very little. Put on your listening face, ensure privacy by removing others, and make sure your whole body looks as though you are paying attention.

○ Make accurate notes about what has been heard, seen or told. Only write down these observations, don't even think of embellishing them in any way or putting any 'slant' on them. Clear, accurate notes will prove crucial to the professionals who may later become involved.

○ Make your concerns known quickly to an appropriate authority, such as the senior designated teacher. Don't waste time. Wasted days mean that the young person may suffer further.

○ Do not discuss concerns with parents unless this is part of an agreed strategy. This is not usually your job and will lead quickly to a deterioration in the teacher–parent relationship. This is especially important if no abuse is found and it may be you who helps to build new bridges between school and home.

○ Do not promise a young person confidentiality about any information on abuse disclosed. This is essential as you will not be able to keep your promise. You could talk about promising to use the information in an appropriate way.

LIST 92 Drugs alert

Drugs are becoming a greater problem as each school year passes. They are now very cheap and readily available. To protect students look out for some of the following changes:

- Dilated pupils
- Scabs around the mouth or nose
- Belligerent behaviour when otherwise relatively normal
- Easily aroused by the slightest thing
- Sudden mood swings
- Asleep or drowsy in class
- Increased aggression or irritability
- Giggly and talkative (more than usual)
- Unusually hyperactive
- Loss of appetite
- Increased appetite
- Sudden group of new friends
- Sudden wealth – the student may be 'dealing' and be able to buy new, expensive things
- Loss of personal belongings.

These are not definite signs of drug use or 'dealing', so do not jump to conclusions but seek help and support as quickly as possible.

Top tip: Look out for changes in students.

Dealing with Parents and Difficult Situations

15

LIST 93 Contacting parents

Sometimes it is necessary to contact parents by phone regarding their child's behaviour in school. Here are some tips to make it easier.

○ Before you make contact, try to find out about the family circumstances – there may be some highly emotive issues or extenuating circumstances.

○ Do it as soon as it becomes necessary – don't put it off.

○ Keep it brief – 30 seconds is long enough as attention spans are short and you need to make an impact.

○ Prepare your message in advance and practise what you intend to say.

○ Identify one clear objective.

○ Decide whether it should be put as a question or a statement.

○ Identify what emotions and demands it might provoke in the parent.

○ Expand the message, giving who, when, where, what, why, how.

○ Link the message to a concrete idea, perhaps a metaphor or simile.

○ Identify what you want the parent to do, e.g. take action.

LIST 94 Giving advice to parents

On occasions such as parents' evenings you may be asked by parents for advice on how to control or modify behaviour. More importantly, you may wish to discuss positive behavioural approaches with certain parents. Such advice is not always well received, especially if they do not believe there is a problem!

- Discuss your intentions with colleagues first to ensure that there are no mixed messages and that you are not walking into a battlefield.
- Be objective in your report. This is difficult for parents to refute.
- Encourage them to give rewards.
- Discuss possible rewards which fit the family lifestyle and budget.
- Persuade them to use much more praise. Not enough praise is a problem in many households.
- Get them to avoid sanctions – it can be hard to persuade parents used to giving the odd clout.
- Point out the problems of long-term sanctions – they can't be used again!
- Encourage them to talk to their child and use the concept of spending 'quality time' with the child, choosing an activity from a list drawn up by the parent.
- Suggest parents restrict TV viewing by giving alternatives and perhaps encouraging children to earn viewing time.
- Suggest they discuss potential rewards with their child, ensuring that these are not expensive.
- Suggest they reward as quickly as possible following acts of good, changed or acceptable behaviour.
- Again, when parents reward their children, encourage them to say why the reward is being given.
- Even when parents are only praising their child, make sure they tell the child why they are pleased.

Boosting the self-esteem of pupils can be a problem, especially with difficult teenagers, but high self-esteem can encourage responsibility and good behaviour as well as enhance learning. General advice to parents may prove more than a little useful. You might try saying something along the lines of, 'I appreciate you provide Jack with a safe, secure, loving home but he is lacking in confidence.' Then make some of the following points:

- ○ 'Be generous with your praise. I know this is difficult, but try to find things Jack does right or well.'
- ○ 'Try to make Jack feel special to you – even if he seems to resent it he will take the comments on board and appreciate them.'
- ○ 'Can you spend more time with him? Some targeted, high-quality time would be useful.'
- ○ 'Find his strengths and interests and encourage activities which take these into account.'
- ○ 'He feels that everything he does is wrong. Try to be more circumspect and leave him to get it right by himself, only giving help if he asks. This may be frustrating for all of you, but would be good for him.'
- ○ 'Give Jack jobs to do so that he feels important and as if he contributes to family life.'
- ○ 'Involve him in family decisions in an appropriate way.'
- ○ 'Above all, try to avoid criticism and be as positive as possible. This is not easy with Jack but at this stage it is essential.'

- ○ Hear parents out first – wait until they calm down.
- ○ Try to say positive things about their child.
- ○ Remember to concentrate on the behaviour, not the child.
- ○ Keep calm and don't retaliate, despite your feelings.
- ○ Keep a reasonable physical distance, just in case.
- ○ Don't raise your voice.
- ○ Don't wag or point your finger.
- ○ Put your points across assertively but calmly.
- ○ Don't be flippant.
- ○ Avoid sarcasm.
- ○ Remember, they may not have all the information – they may believe everything their child tells them.
- ○ Seek help or support if you feel threatened in any way.
- ○ Offer to get a more senior member of staff.
- ○ Agree to differ if you are not making progress, and suggest meeting at a later date.

LIST 97 Resolving conflict

Whether you are dealing with an irate parent or another person at
school who for some reason has issues with you, there are some
steps you can take to rescue the situation.

Keep a sense of perspective

- ○ Think positively.
- ○ Remember, it's probably not personal but about the school or
  even your subject.
- ○ Seek a sense of partnership with the person about the problem.
- ○ Learn to notice the early warning signs of your own emotional
  arousal.
- ○ Take deep breaths and keep relaxed.

Give your full attention to the person

- ○ Give good, relaxed eye contact but it's not a good idea to
  outstare them.
- ○ Listen carefully.
- ○ Try to see the problem from their point of view.
- ○ Make notes to clarify the situation – they may prove very useful
  later.
- ○ Don't interrupt.

Check your understanding of their problem

- ○ Recap the content with them.
- ○ Recap their feelings with them.
- ○ Learn more by asking questions if necessary.

Find agreement

- ○ Agree that they are in the right, or
- ○ Agree with the frustration they must be feeling.

Move to action

- ○ Deal with the problem.
- ○ Find out more or move on.
- ○ If the person remains irate, start again.

Delay

- If you need more time to sort out the problem, keep them informed, say when you will get back to them and deliver your promise.
- If someone else is going to deal with the problem, clarify this with both parties and pass on any notes and comments.

Confront

- Make the person aware of what they are doing, e.g. 'I've made some suggestions for what we might do to put things right, but I can see that you're still annoyed. Is there some way in which we can solve this problem together?' or 'Would you prefer to deal with someone else?'
- If the other person becomes abusive, walk away and get help or support.

LIST 98 Assessing aggression and potential violence

Occasionally a parent or visitor to the school may prove to be aggressive or even violent. Visitors without the agreed school identification should always be challenged but be wary and make sure you can recognize any danger signs.

Assess the danger. Does the person have (to your knowledge):

- high levels of stress
- a drink problem
- a drug problem
- a history of violence
- any criminal convictions
- a psychiatric illness?

Has this person:

- verbally abused you before
- threatened you with violence before
- attacked you before
- perceived you as a threat to their child
- got unrealistic expectations of what you can do for them or their child
- previously viewed you as deliberately obstructive?

Ask yourself:

- are there other people around who may encourage or reward violence
- are colleagues aware of your whereabouts
- are you able to attract attention if attacked
- are you likely to be trapped if attacked
- what would you do if attacked?

LIST 99 — What to do about difficult situations

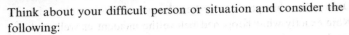

Think about your difficult person or situation and consider the following:

- What actually happens that you find difficult? Be as specific as you can.
- How often does it occur?
- How long does it last?
- What impact does it have on you and any others who happen to be around at the time?
- What triggers the problem? What leads up to it, what do others do, and what happens as a result?
- How do you feel when this bad behaviour happens?
- Why do you think the person behaves in this way?

Are any of the following options open to you?

- Can you change any of the things that lead up to the problem?
- Can you change what you do?
- Can you challenge the situation directly or even confront the difficult behaviour?
- Can you change the consequences in any way?
- Can you build any kind of bridge between you and the other person?
- Is it possible for you to change your view about what is happening and the difficult behaviour?
- Can someone else help you with any of these?

Remember, this can apply to situations with other staff or parents and not just students.

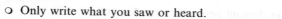

LIST 100 Reporting incidents

- Only write what you saw or heard.
- Note exactly what happened before the incident as well as the incident itself and what happened afterwards.
- Don't report hearsay.
- Be brief and accurate.
- Be objective about your personal feelings.
- Try to leave your prejudices behind.
- Note the consequences of any actions by you or the student.
- Write about the precedents – think carefully about what could have triggered the behaviour – but only report the facts, not your guesses.
- Report who else was around, e.g. students and staff.
- Report whether any first-aid was required by either party or any bystanders.
- Note the time and date of the incident and be sure to date your report.
- Use simple language.
- If it is a serious incident, keep a copy.

Top tip: Work on polishing up your skills – we all continue to learn.

LIST 101 Top-tip summary

- However good you are you can always be better.
- Never ever criticize the person, only the behaviour.
- Remember: rights lead to responsibilities which lead to the need for rules.
- Be well prepared and prepared to change.
- Remember to give choice and take-up time – essential for avoiding and dealing with any trouble.
- Never wade in when a lower-level strategy will suffice.
- Always try to use positive language, even when commenting on poor behaviour.
- Good teaching is the best solution; reward systems work and sanctions are the least effective.
- There are others there to help you.
- Avoid or remove audiences when dealing with difficult situations.
- Be alert to small events that could potentially spark greater difficulties.
- Whatever your mood, look calm, cool and collected, even if you don't feel it.
- For those special children, seek advice and read the paperwork.
- Look out for changes in students.
- Work on polishing up your skills – we all continue to learn.